Diaper Covers & Caps™

General Information

Many of the products used in this pattern book can be purchased from local craft, fabric and variety stores, or from the Annie's Attic Needlecraft Catalog (see Customer Service information on page 32).

Contents

Ruffles

SKILL LEVEL

INTERMEDIATE

FINISHED SIZES

Newborn–3 months, 3–6 months and 9 months–1 year

MATERIALS

- Cascade Yarn Fixation fine (sport) weight elastic yarn (1¾ oz/100 yds/50g per ball):
  - 2 balls #8001 opulent white
  - 1 ball #3077 pink lemonade
- Size crochet hook needed for size and gauge
- Tapestry needle

2 FINE

GAUGE

Newborn–3 months, size C/2/2.75mm hook: 7 dc = 1 inch

3–6 months, size D/3/3.25mm hook: 6 dc = 1 inch

9 months–1 year, size E/4/3.5mm: 5 dc = 1 inch

Take time to check gauge.

PATTERN NOTES

If using a different yarn, make sure it will stretch and also hold original shape and size, in order to fit properly over diaper.

Chain-2 at beginning of row or round counts as first double crochet unless otherwise stated.

Join with slip stitch as indicated unless otherwise stated.

INSTRUCTIONS
DIAPER COVER
BACK
RIBBING

Row 1: With pink lemonade, ch 9, sc in 2nd ch from hook and in each ch across, turn. *(8 sc)*

Rows 2–54: Working in **back lps** *(see Stitch Guide)*, ch 1, sc in each st across, turn. At end of last row, **do not turn.**

BODY

Row 1: Working in ends of rows on Ribbing, ch 1, sc in each row across, turn. *(54 sc)*

Row 2: Working in both lps, ch 1, sc in each of first 8 sts, 2 sc in next st, [sc in each of next 8 sts, 2 sc in next st] across, turn. *(60 sc)*

Row 3: **Ch 2** *(see Pattern Notes)*, dc in each st across, turn.

Row 4: Ch 1, sc in each st across, turn.

Rows 5–7: [Rep rows 3 and 4 alternately] twice, ending last rep with row 3.

Row 8: Working in back lps, rep row 4.

Rows 9–11: [Rep rows 3 and 4 alternately] twice, ending last rep with row 3.

Row 12: Working in back lps, rep row 4.

Rows 13–15: [Rep rows 3 and 4 alternately] twice, ending last rep with row 3.

Row 16: Working in back lps, sk first st, loosely sl st in each of next 2 sts, sc in each of next 54 sts, leaving rem sts unworked, turn. *(54 sc)*

Rows 17–23: Sk first st, loosely sl st in each of next 2 sts, sc in each st across, leaving last 3 sc unworked, turn. *(12 sc at end of last row)*

Rows 24–32: Ch 1, sc in each st across, turn. At end of last row, fasten off.

RUFFLE

Row 1: With Ribbing at bottom and working in rem lps of row 7, **join** *(see Pattern Notes)* opulent white in first st, ch 2, 2 dc in same st, 3 dc in each st across, turn.

Row 2: Ch 2, dc in each st across, turn.

Row 3: (Ch 1, sc) in each st across. Fasten off.

Rep Ruffle in rem lps of row 11 and row 15.

FRONT
RIBBING

Row 1: With pink lemonade, ch 9, sc in 2nd ch from hook and in each ch across, turn. *(8 sc)*

Rows 2–18: Working in back lps, ch 1, sc in each st across, turn. At end of last row, **do not turn.**

BODY

Row 1: Working in ends of rows on Ribbing, ch 1, sc in each row across, turn. *(18 sc)*

Row 2: Ch 1, sc in each of first 5 sts, 2 sc in next st, [sc in each of next 5 sts, 2 sc in next st] across, turn. *(21 sc)*

Rows 3–15: [Rep rows 3 and 4 of Back Body alternately] 7 times, ending last rep with row 3.

Row 16: Ch 1, sc in each st across, turn.

Row 17: Ch 1, **sc dec** *(see Stitch Guide)* in first 2 sts, sc in each st across, ending with sc dec in last 2 sts, turn. *(19 sc)*

Row 18: Ch 1, sc in each st across, turn.

Rows 19–24: [Rep rows 17 and 18 alternately] 3 times. *(13 sc at end of last row)*

Row 25: Ch 1, sc in each of first 6 sts, sc dec in next 2 sts, sc in each st across, turn. *(12 sc)*

Rows 26–32: Ch 1, sc in each st across, turn. At end of last row, fasten off.

ASSEMBLY

Sew side edges of Front to Back from Ribbing to top of row 16 of Body.

Sew last row of Front and Back tog for crotch.

LEG

Rnd 1: With pink lemonade, evenly sp 54 sc around Leg opening, **do not join.**

Rnd 2: Sc in each st around, join in next st. Fasten off.

Rnd 3: Join opulent white with sc in first st, sc in each of next 6 sts, sc dec in next 2 sts, [sc in each of next 7 sts, sc dec in next 2 sts] around. *(48 sc)*

Rnd 4: [Sc in each of next 6 sts, sc dec in next 2 sts] around. *(42 sc)*

Rnds 5 & 6: Sc in each st around.

Rnd 7: Sc in first st, ch 2, sk next st, [sc in next st, ch 2, sk next st] around, join in beg sc. Fasten off.

Rep on rem Leg opening.

RUFFLE HAT

Row 1: With opulent white, ch 73, sc in 2nd ch from hook and in each ch across, turn. *(72 sc)*

Row 2: **Ch 2** *(see Pattern Notes)*, dc in each st across, turn.

Row 3: Working in **back lps** *(see Stitch Guide)*, ch 1, sc in each st across, turn.

Row 4: Ch 2, dc in each st across, turn.

Row 5: Ch 1, sc in each st across, turn.

Rows 6–15: [Rep rows 4 and 5 alternately] 5 times.

Row 16: Rep row 5.

Row 17: Ch 1, sc in each of first 10 sts, **sc dec** *(see Stitch Guide)* in next 2 sts, [sc in each of next 10 sts, sc dec in next 2 sts] across, turn. *(66 sc)*

Row 18: Ch 2, dc in each of next 8 sts, **dc dec** *(see Stitch Guide)* in next 2 sts, [dc in each of next 9 sts, dc dec in next 2 sts] across, turn. *(60 dc)*

Row 19: Ch 1, sc in each of first 8 sts, sc dec in next 2 sts, [sc in each of next 8 sts, sc dec in next 2 sts] across, turn. *(54 sc)*

Row 20: Ch 2, dc in each of next 6 sts, dc dec in next 2 sts, [dc in each of next 7 sts, dc dec in next 2 sts] across, turn. *(48 dc)*

Row 21: Ch 1, sc in each of first 6 sts, sc dec in next 2 sts, [sc in each of next 6 sts, sc dec in next 2 sts] across, turn. *(42 sc)*

Row 22: Ch 2, dc in each of next 4 sts, dc dec in next 2 sts, [dc in each of next 5 sts, dc dec in next 2 sts] across, turn. *(36 dc)*

Row 23: Ch 1, sc in each of first 4 sts, sc dec in next 2 sts, [sc in each of next 4 sts, sc dec in next 2 sts] across, turn. *(30 sc)*

Row 24: Ch 2, dc in each of next 2 sts, dc dec in next 2 sts, [dc in each of next 3 sts, dc dec in next 2 sts] across, turn. *(24 dc)*

Row 25: Ch 1, sc in each of first 2 sts, sc dec in next 2 sts, [sc in each of next 2 sts, sc dec in next 2 sts] across, turn. *(18 sc)*

Row 26: Ch 2, dc dec in next 2 sts, [dc in next st, dc dec in next 2 sts] across, turn. *(12 dc)*

Row 27: Ch 1, [sc dec in next 2 sts] across. Leaving long end, fasten off.

Weave long end through top of sts on last row, pull to close. Secure end.

RUFFLE

Row 1: With bottom edge away from you, join opulent white in any rem lp of rnd 2, ch 2, dc in same st, 2 dc in each st across, turn.

Rows 2 & 3: Ch 2, dc in each st across, turn. At end of last row, fasten off.

Turn rows 1 and 2 of Ruffle Hat to WS and sew in place.

Sew ends of rows tog for back seam.

FLOWER

Rnd 1: With pink lemonade, ch 2, 6 sc in 2nd ch from hook, **do not join.** *(6 sc)*

Rnd 2: 2 sc in each st around. *(12 sc)*

Rnd 3: [Sl st in next st, ch 1, hdc in same st, 2 dc in next st, (hdc, ch 1, sl st) in next st] around. *(6 petals)*

Rnd 4: [Working behind petals, ch 3, sl st between next 2 petals] around.

Rnd 5: (Sc, hdc, dc, tr, dc, hdc, sc) in each ch-3 sp around, join in beg sc. Fasten off.

Sew to Hat as shown in photo. ■

Sail Away

SKILL LEVEL

INTERMEDIATE

FINISHED SIZES

Newborn–3 months, 3–6 months and 9 months–1 year

MATERIALS

- Cascade Yarn Fixation fine (sport) weight elastic yarn (1¾ oz/100 yds/50g per ball):
  2 balls #9045 stonewash
  1 ball each #8001 opulent white, #9398 hot pink and #1198 light yellow
- Size 3 pearl cotton:
  1 yd each red, brown and black
- Size crochet hook needed for size and gauge
- Tapestry needle
- Stitch marker

2 FINE

GAUGE

Newborn–3 months, size C/2/2.75mm hook: 7 dc = 1 inch
3–6 months, size D/3/3.25mm hook: 6 dc = 1 inch
9 months–1 year, size E/4/3.5mm: 5 dc = 1 inch
Take time to check gauge.

PATTERN NOTES

If using a different yarn, make sure it will stretch and also hold original shape and size, in order to fit properly over diaper.

Chain-2 at beginning of row or round counts as first double crochet unless otherwise stated.

Join with slip stitch as indicated unless otherwise stated.

Work in continuous rounds, do not turn or join unless otherwise stated.

Mark first stitch of round.

INSTRUCTIONS

DIAPER COVER

BACK

RIBBING

Row 1: With stonewash, ch 9, sc in 2nd ch from hook and in each ch across, turn. *(8 sc)*

Rows 2–54: Working in **back lps** *(see Stitch Guide)*, ch 1, sc in each st across, turn. At end of last row, **do not turn**.

BODY

Row 1: Working in ends of rows on Ribbing, ch 1, sc in each row across, turn. *(54 sc)*

Row 2: Working in both lps, ch 1, sc in each of first 8 sts, 2 sc in next st, [sc in each of next 8 sts, 2 sc in next st] across, turn. *(60 sc)*

Row 3: **Ch 2** *(see Pattern Notes)*, dc in each st across, turn.

Row 4: Ch 1, sc in each st across, turn.

Rows 5–14: [Rep rows 3 and 4 alternately] 5 times.

Row 15: Rep row 3.

Row 16: Sk first st, sl st loosely in each of next 2 sc, sc in next st and in each across, leaving last 3 sts unworked, turn. *(54 sc)*

Rows 17–23: Sk first st, sl st in each of next 2 sts, sc in next st and in each st across, leaving last 3 sts unworked, turn. *(12 sc at end of last row)*

Rows 24–32: Ch 1, sc in each st across, turn. At end of last row, fasten off.

FRONT

RIBBING

Row 1: With stonewash, ch 9, sc in 2nd ch from hook and in each ch across, turn. *(8 sc)*

Rows 2–18: Working in back lps, ch 1, sc in each st across, turn. At end of last row, **do not turn**.

BODY

Row 1: Working in ends of rows on Ribbing, ch 1, sc in each row across, turn. *(18 sc)*

Row 2: Ch 1, sc in each of first 5 sts, 2 sc in next st, [sc in each of next 5 sts, 2 sc in next st] across, turn. *(21 sc)*

Rows 3–15: [Rep rows 3 and 4 of Back Body alternately] 7 times, ending last rep with row 3.

Row 16: Ch 1, sc in each st across, turn.

Row 17: Ch 1, **sc dec** *(see Stitch Guide)* in first 2 sts, sc in each st across, ending with sc dec in last 2 sts, turn. *(19 sc)*

Row 18: Ch 1, sc in each st across, turn.

Rows 19–24: [Rep rows 17 and 18 alternately] 3 times. *(13 sc at end of last row)*

Row 25: Ch 1, sc in each of first 6 sts, sc dec in next 2 sts, sc in each st across, turn. *(12 sc)*

Rows 26–32: Ch 1, sc in each st across, turn. At end of last row, fasten off.

ASSEMBLY

Sew side edges of Front to Back from Ribbing to top of row 16 of Body.

Sew last row of Front and Back tog for crotch.

LEG

Rnd 1: With stonewash, evenly sp 54 sc around Leg opening, **do not join** *(see Pattern Notes)*.

Rnd 2: Sc in each st around, join in next st. Fasten off.

Rnd 3: Join light yellow with sc in first st, sc in each of next 6 sts, sc dec in next 2 sts, [sc in each of next 7 sts, sc dec in next 2 sts] around. *(48 sc)*

Rnd 4: [Sc in each of next 6 sts, sc dec in next 2 sts] around. *(42 sc)*

Rnds 5–7: Sc in each st around.

At end of last rnd, join in next st. Fasten off.

Rep on rem Leg opening.

LARGE SAIL

Row 1: With opulent white, ch 8, sc in 2nd ch from hook, and in each ch across, turn. *(7 sc)*

Row 2: Ch 1, sc in each of first 5 sts, sc dec in last 2 sts, turn. *(6 sc)*

Row 3: Ch 1, sc in each st across, turn.

Row 4: Ch 1, sc in each of first 4 sts, sc dec in last 2 sts, turn. *(5 sc)*

Row 5: Ch 1, sc in each st across, turn.

Row 6: Ch 1, sc in each of first 3 sts, sc dec in last 2 sts, turn. *(4 sc)*

Row 7: Ch 1, sc in each st across, turn.

Row 8: Ch 1, sc in each of first 2 sts, sc dec in last 2 sts, turn. *(3 sc)*

Row 9: Ch 1, sc in each st across, turn.

Row 10: Ch 1, sc in first st, sc dec in last 2 sts, turn. *(2 sc)*

Row 11: Ch 1, sc dec in 2 sts. Fasten off.

SMALL SAIL

Row 1: With white, ch 5, sc in 2nd ch from hook, and in each ch across, turn. *(4 sc)*

Row 2: Ch 1, sc in each of first 2 sts, sc dec in last 2 sts, turn. *(3 sc)*

Row 3: Ch 1, sc in each st across, turn.

Row 4: Ch 1, sc in first st, sc dec in last 2 sts, turn. *(2 sc)*

Row 5: Ch 1, sc dec in 2 sts. Fasten off.

BOAT

Row 1: With hot pink, ch 16, sc in 2nd ch from hook and in each ch across, turn. *(15 sc)*

Rows 2 & 3: Ch 1, sc dec in first 2 sts, sc in each st across with sc dec in last 2 sts, turn. At end of last row, fasten off. *(11 sc at end of last row)*

ASSEMBLY

Sew Sails in place in center of Back on Cover as shown in photo.

Using **chain stitch** *(see Fig. 1)*, with brown pearl cotton, embroider pole as shown in photo.

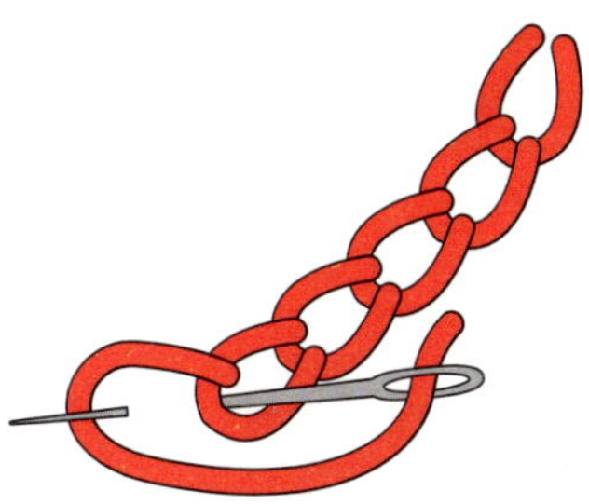

Fig. 1
Chain Stitch

Using **satin stitch** *(see Fig. 2)*, with red pearl cotton, embroider flag at top of pole.

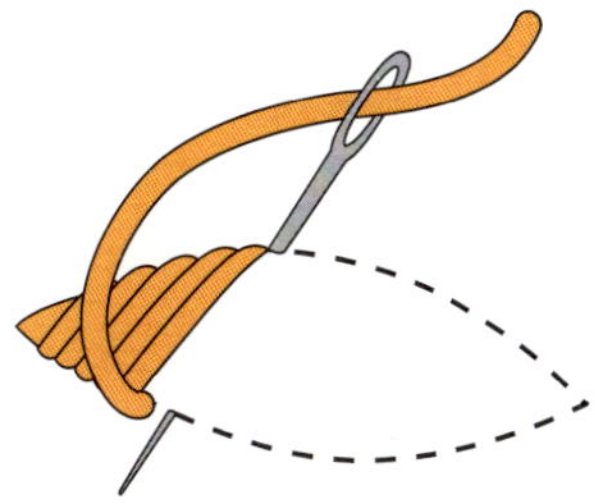

Fig. 2
Satin Stitch

Sew Boat below Sails as shown in photo.

SAIL AWAY HAT

Row 1: With stonewash, ch 79, sc in 2nd ch from hook and in each ch across, turn. *(78 sc)*

Rows 2–9: Ch 1, sc in each st across, turn.

Row 10: Fold up row 1 to back of work, working through all thicknesses of row 1 and row 9 at same time, ch 1, sc in each st across, turn.

Row 11: Ch 1, sc in each of first 11 sts, **sc dec** *(see Stitch Guide)* in next 2 sts, [sc in each of next 11 sts, sc dec in next 2 sts] across, turn. *(72 sc)*

Row 12: **Ch 2** *(see Pattern Notes)*, dc in each st across, turn.

Row 13: Ch 1, sc in each st across, turn.

Rows 14–22: [Rep rows 12 and 13 alternately] 4 times, ending last rep with row 12.

Row 23: Ch 1, sc in each of first 10 sts, sc dec in next 2 sts, [sc in each of next 10 sts, sc dec in next 2 sts] across. *(66 sc)*

Row 24: Ch 2, dc in each of next 8 sts, **dc dec** *(see Stitch Guide)* in next 2 sts, [dc in each of next 9 sts, dc dec in next 2 sts] across. *(60 dc)*

Row 25: Ch 1, sc in each of first 8 sts, sc dec in next 2 sts, [sc in each of next 8 sts, sc dec in next 2 sts] across. *(54 sc)*

Row 26: Ch 2, dc in each of next 6 sts, dc dec in next 2 sts, [dc in each of next 7 sts, dc dec in next 2 sts] across. *(48 dc)*

Row 27: Ch 1, sc in each of first 6 sts, sc dec in next 2 sts, [sc in each of next 6 sts, sc dec in next 2 sts] across. *(42 sc)*

Row 28: Ch 2, dc in each of next 4 sts, dc dec in next 2 sts, [dc in each of next 5 sts, dc dec in next 2 sts] across. *(36 dc)*

Row 29: Ch 1, sc in each of first 4 sts, sc dec in next 2 sts, [sc in each of next 4 sts, sc dec in next 2 sts] across. *(30 sc)*

Row 30: Ch 2, dc in each of next 2 sts, dc dec in next 2 sts, [dc in each of next 3 sts, dc dec in next 2 sts] across. *(24 dc)*

Row 31: Ch 1, sc in each of first 2 sts, sc dec in next 2 sts, [sc in each of next 2 sts, sc dec in next 2 sts] across. *(18 sc)*

Row 32: Ch 1, sc in each st across, turn.

Row 33: Ch 1, sc in first st, sc dec in next 2 sts, [sc in next st, sc dec in next 2 sts] across, turn. *(12 sc)*

Rows 34–36: Ch 1, sc in each st across, turn.

Row 37: Ch 1, sc dec in first 2 sts, [sc dec in next 2 sts] across, turn. *(6 sc)*

Row 38: Ch 1, sc in each st across, turn.

Row 39: Ch 1, sc dec in first 2 sts, [sc dec in next 2 sts] across. Leaving long end, fasten off. *(3 sc)*

Weave long end through sts on last row, pull to close. Secure end.

Sew ends of rows tog.

SUN

Rnd 1: With light yellow, ch 2, 6 sc in 2nd ch from hook, **do not join.**

Rnd 2: 2 sc in each st around. *(12 sc)*

Rnd 3: [Sc in next st, 2 sc in next st] around. *(18 sc)*

Rnd 4: [Sc in each of next 2 sts, 2 sc in next st] around. *(24 sc)*

Rnd 5: [Sc in each of next 3 sts, 2 sc in next st] around. *(30 sc)*

Rnd 6: [Sc in each of next 4 sts, 2 sc in next st] around. *(36 sc)*

Rnd 7: *Sl st in next st, ch 5, sl st in 2nd ch from hook, sc in next ch, hdc in next ch, dc in last ch, sk next 2 sts on last rnd, rep from * around, join in beg sl st. Fasten off.

FINISHING

Using **French knots** *(see Fig. 3)*, with black pearl cotton, embroider eyes on Sun ¾ inch apart as shown in photo.

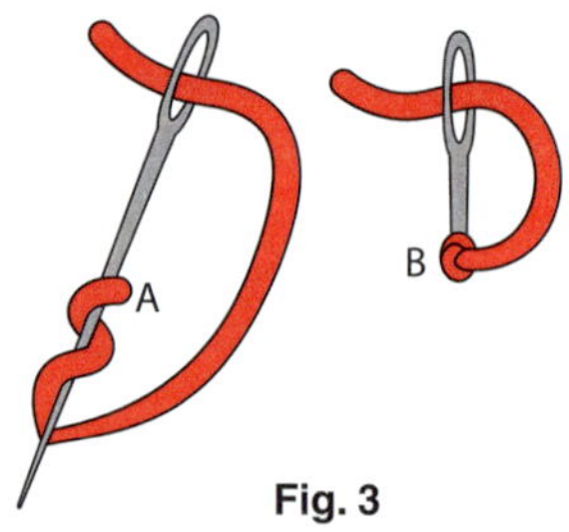

Fig. 3
French Knot

Using **straight stitch** *(see Fig. 4)*, with black pearl cotton, embroider nose centered below eyes, and mouth centered below nose, as shown in photo.

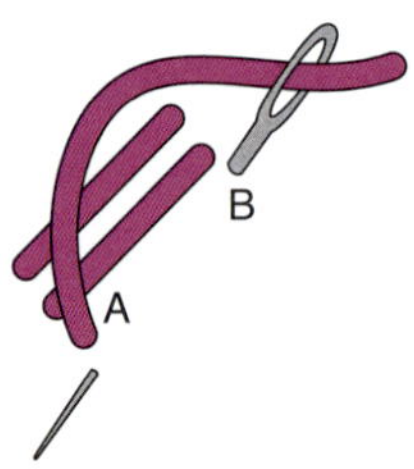

Fig. 4
Straight Stitch

Sew Sun on Sail Away Hat. ■

Froggie

SKILL LEVEL

INTERMEDIATE

FINISHED SIZES

Newborn–3 months, 3–6 months and 9 months–1 year

MATERIALS

- Cascade Yarn Fixation fine (sport) weight elastic yarn (1¾ oz/ 100 yds/50g per ball):
  - 2 balls #9398 hot pink
  - 1 ball each #8001 opulent white and #5800 moss
- Size 3 pearl cotton:
  - 1 yd each red and black
- Size crochet hook needed for size and gauge
- Tapestry needle
- Fiberfill
- Stitch marker

2 FINE

GAUGE

Newborn–3 months, size C/2/2.75mm hook: 7 dc = 1 inch

3–6 months, size D/3/3.25mm hook: 6 dc = 1 inch

9 months–1 year, size E/4/3.5mm: 5 dc = 1 inch

Take time to check gauge.

PATTERN NOTES

If using a different yarn, make sure it will stretch and also hold original shape and size, in order to fit properly over diaper.

Chain-2 at beginning of row or round counts as first double crochet unless otherwise stated.

Join with slip stitch as indicated unless otherwise stated.

Work in continuous rounds, do not turn or join unless otherwise stated.

Mark first stitch of round.

INSTRUCTIONS
DIAPER COVER
BACK
RIBBING

Row 1: With hot pink, ch 9, sc in 2nd ch from hook and in each ch across, turn. *(8 sc)*

Rows 2–54: Working in **back lps** *(see Stitch Guide)*, ch 1, sc in each st across, turn. At end of last row, **do not turn.**

BODY

Row 1: Working in ends of rows on Ribbing, ch 1, sc in each row across, turn. *(54 sc)*

Row 2: Working in both lps, ch 1, sc in each of first 8 sts, 2 sc in next st, [sc in each of next 8 sts, 2 sc in next st] across, turn. *(60 sc)*

Row 3: Ch 2 *(see Pattern Notes)*, dc in each st across, turn.

Row 4: Ch 1, sc in each st across, turn.

Rows 5–14: [Rep rows 3 and 4 alternately] 5 times.

Row 15: Rep row 3.

Row 16: Sk first st, sl st loosely in each of next 2 sc, sc in next st and in each across, leaving last 3 sts unworked, turn. *(54 sc)*

Rows 17–23: Sk first st, sl st in each of next 2 sts, sc in next st and in each st across, leaving last 3 sts unworked, turn. *(12 sc at end of last row)*

Rows 24–32: Ch 1, sc in each st across, turn. At end of last row, fasten off.

FRONT
RIBBING

Row 1: With hot pink, ch 9, sc in 2nd ch from hook and in each ch across, turn. *(8 sc)*

Rows 2–18: Working in back lps, ch 1, sc in each st across, turn. At end of last row, **do not turn.**

BODY

Row 1: Working in ends of rows on Ribbing, ch 1, sc in each row across, turn. *(18 sc)*

Row 2: Ch 1, sc in each of first 5 sts, 2 sc in next st, [sc in each of next 5 sts, 2 sc in next st] across, turn. *(21 sc)*

Rows 3–15: [Rep rows 3 and 4 of Back Body alternately] 7 times, ending last rep with row 3.

Row 16: Ch 1, sc in each st across, turn.

Row 17: Ch 1, **sc dec** *(see Stitch Guide)* in first 2 sts, sc in each st across, ending with sc dec in last 2 sts, turn. *(19 sc)*

Row 18: Ch 1, sc in each st across, turn.

Rows 19–24: [Rep rows 17 and 18 alternately] 3 times. *(13 sc at end of last row)*

Row 25: Ch 1, sc in each of first 6 sts, sc dec in next 2 sts, sc in each st across, turn. *(12 sc)*

Rows 26–32: Ch 1, sc in each st across, turn. At end of last row, fasten off.

ASSEMBLY

Sew side edges of Front to Back from Ribbing to top of row 16 of Body.

Sew last row of Front and Back tog for crotch.

LEG

Rnd 1: Join *(see Pattern Notes)* hot pink at seam, evenly sp 54 sc around Leg opening, join in beg sc. Fasten off.

Rnd 2: Join opulent white with sc in first st, sc in each st around, **do not join** *(see Pattern Notes).*

Rnd 3: [Sc in each of next 7 sts, sc dec in next 2 sts] around, join in next st. Fasten off. *(48 sc)*

Rnd 4: Join moss with sc in first st, sc in each of next 5 sts, sc dec in next 2 sts, [sc in each of next 6 sts, sc dec in next 2 sts] around. *(42 sc)*

Rnd 5: Sc in each st around, join in next st. Fasten off.

Rnd 6: Join opulent white with sc in first st, sc in each st around.

Rnds 7 & 8: Sc in each st around.

At end of last rnd, join in next st. Fasten off.

Rep on rem Leg opening.

PATCH

Row 1: With opulent white, ch 22, sc in 2nd ch from hook and in each ch across, turn. *(21 sc)*

Row 2: Ch 2, dc in each st across, turn.

Row 3: Ch 1, sc in each st across, turn.

Rows 4–15: [Rep rows 2 and 3 alternately] 6 times. At end of last row, fasten off.

FROG

HEAD

Rnd 1: With moss, ch 2, 6 sc in 2nd ch from hook, **do not join.** *(6 sc)*

Rnd 2: 2 sc in each st around. *(12 sc)*

Rnd 3: [Sc in next st, 2 sc in next st] around. *(18 sc)*

Rnd 4: [Sc in each of next 2 sts, 2 sc in next st] around. *(24 sc)*

Row 5: Sl st in next st, ch 1, 4 dc in next st, ch 1, sl st in each of next 5 sts, ch 1, 4 dc in next st, ch 1, sl st in next st, leaving rem sts unworked. Fasten off.

EYE
MAKE 2.

With opulent white, ch 2, 6 sc in 2nd ch from hook, join in beg sc. Fasten off.

FINISHING

Using **French knot** *(see Fig. 1)*, with black pearl cotton, embroider 1 French knot in each Eye.

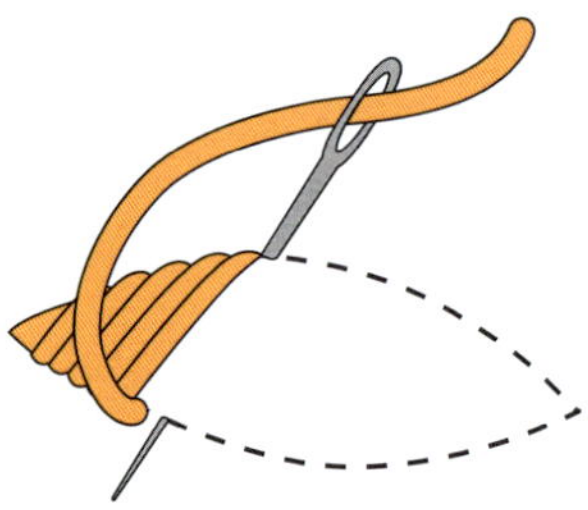

Fig. 1
Satin Stitch

Sew Eyes to dc sts on last rnd of Head as shown in photo.

Using **couching stitch** *(see Fig. 2)*, with red pearl cotton, embroider mouth centered below Eyes.

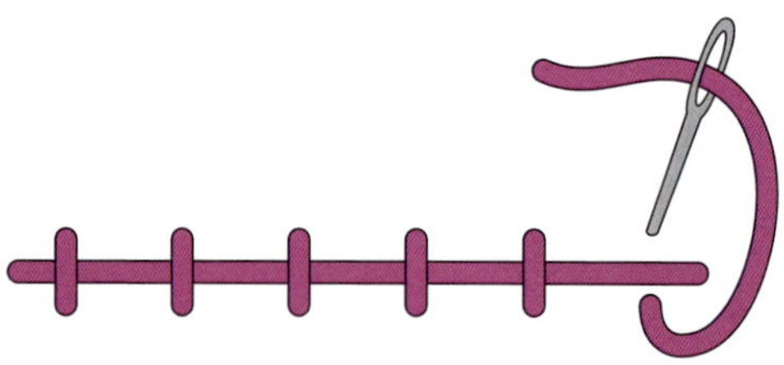

Fig. 2
Couching Stitch

BODY

Rnd 1: With moss, ch 2, 6 sc in 2nd ch from hook, **do not join**. *(6 sc)*

Rnd 2: 2 sc in each st around. *(12 sc)*

Rnd 3: [Sc in next st, 2 sc in next st] around. *(18 sc)*

Rnd 4: [Sc in each of next 2 sts, 2 sc in next st] around. *(24 sc)*

Rnd 5: [Sc in each of next 3 sts, 2 sc in next st] around. *(30 sc)*

Rnd 6: [Sc in each of next 4 sts, 2 sc in next st] around, join in next st. Fasten off.

ASSEMBLY

Sew Body to bottom center of Patch, stuffing very lightly with fiberfill.

Sew Head on Patch, slightly overlapping top edge of Body and stuffing very lightly with fiberfill.

Sew Patch to center Back of Diaper Cover.

FLOWER
MAKE 3.

With opulent white, ch 4, sl st in first ch to form ring, [ch 1, 3 dc in ring, ch 1, sc in ring] 4 times. Fasten off.

Sew in place on Front of Diaper Cover as shown in photo.

HAT
RIBBING

Row 1: With hot pink, ch 13, sc in 2nd ch from hook and in each ch across, turn. *(12 sc)*

Rows 2–78: Working in **back lps** *(see Stitch Guide)*, ch 1, sc in each st across, turn. At end of last row, **do not turn**.

TOP SECTION

Row 1: Working in ends of rows, ch 1, sc in each row across, turn. Fasten off. *(78 sc)*

Row 2: Join opulent white in first st, ch 2, dc in each st across, turn.

Row 3: Ch 1, sc in each st across, turn. Fasten off.

Row 4: Join moss in first st, ch 2, dc in each st across, turn. Fasten off.

Row 5: Join opulent white with sc in first st, sc in each st across, turn.

Row 6: **Ch 2** *(see Pattern Notes)*, dc in each st across, turn.

Row 7: Ch 1, sc in each st across, turn. Fasten off.

Row 8: Join hot pink in first st, ch 2, dc in each st across, turn.

Row 9: Ch 1, sc in each st across, turn.

Row 10: Ch 2, dc in each st across, turn.

Row 11: Ch 1, sc in each st across, turn.

Row 12: Ch 2, dc in each of next 10 sts, **dc dec** *(see Stitch Guide)* in next 2 sts, [dc in each of next 11 sts, dc dec in next 2 sts] across, turn. *(72 dc)*

Row 13: Ch 1, sc in each of first 10 sts, **sc dec** *(see Stitch Guide)* in next 2 sts, [sc in each of next 10 sts, sc dec in next 2 sts] across, turn. *(66 sc)*

Row 14: Ch 2, dc in each of next 8 sts, dc dec in next 2 sts, [dc in each of next 9 sts, dc dec in next 2 sts] across, turn. *(60 dc)*

Row 15: Ch 1, sc in each of first 8 sts, sc dec in next 2 sts, [sc in each of next 8 sts, sc dec in next 2 sts] across, turn. *(54 sc)*

Row 16: Ch 2, dc in each of next 6 sts, dc dec in next 2 sts, [dc in each of next 7 sts, dc dec in next 2 sts] across, turn. *(48 dc)*

Row 17: Ch 1, sc in each of first 6 sts, sc dec in next 2 sts, [sc in each of next 6 sts, sc dec in next 2 sts] across, turn. *(42 sc)*

Row 18: Ch 2, dc in each of next 4 sts, dc dec in next 2 sts, [dc in each of next 5 sts, dc dec in next 2 sts] across, turn. *(36 dc)*

Row 19: Ch 1, sc in each of first 4 sts, sc dec in next 2 sts, [sc in each of next 4 sts, sc dec in next 2 sts] across, turn. *(30 sc)*

Row 20: Ch 2, dc in each of next 2 sts, dc dec in next 2 sts, [dc in each of next 3 sts, dc dec in next 2 sts] across, turn. *(24 dc)*

Row 21: Ch 1, sc in each of first 2 sts, sc dec in next 2 sts, [sc in each of next 2 sts, sc dec in next 2 sts] across, turn. *(18 sc)*

Row 22: Ch 2, dc dec in next 2 sts, [dc in next st, dc dec in next 2 sts] across, turn. *(12 dc)*

Row 23: Ch 1, [sc dec in next 2 sts] across. Leaving long end, fasten off.

Weave long end through top of sts on last row, pull to close. Secure end.

Sew ends of rows tog for back seam.

FROG

Work Head, Eyes and Finishing same as Frog Head on Diaper Cover.

Sew to Hat as shown in photo, very lightly stuffing with fiberfill. ■

Little Flapper

SKILL LEVEL

INTERMEDIATE

FINISHED SIZES

Newborn–3 months, 3–6 months and 9 months–1 year

MATERIALS

- Cascade Yarn Fixation fine (sport) weight elastic yarn (1¾ oz/100 yds/50g per ball):
  3 balls #9946 Easter
- Size crochet hook needed for size and gauge
- Tapestry needle
- Stitch marker

GAUGE

Newborn–3 months, size C/2/2.75mm hook: 7 dc = 1 inch
3–6 months, size D/3/3.25mm hook: 6 dc = 1 inch
9 months–1 year, size E/4/3.5mm: 5 dc = 1 inch
Take time to check gauge.

PATTERN NOTES

If using a different yarn, make sure it will stretch and also hold original shape and size, in order to fit properly over diaper.

Chain-2 at beginning of row or round counts as first double crochet unless otherwise stated.

Join with slip stitch as indicated unless otherwise stated.

Work in continuous rounds, do not turn or join unless otherwise stated.

Mark first stitch of round.

INSTRUCTIONS
DIAPER COVER
BACK
RIBBING

Row 1: Ch 9, sc in 2nd ch from hook and in each ch across, turn. *(8 sc)*

Rows 2–54: Working in **back lps** *(see Stitch Guide)*, ch 1, sc in each st across, turn. At end of last row, **do not turn**.

BODY

Row 1: Working in ends of rows on Ribbing, ch 1, sc in each row across, turn. *(54 sc)*

Row 2: Working in both lps, ch 1, sc in each of first 8 sts, 2 sc in next st, [sc in each of next 8 sts, 2 sc in next st] across, turn. *(60 sc)*

Row 3: **Ch 2** *(see Pattern Notes)*, dc in each st across, turn.

Row 4: Ch 1, sc in each st across, turn.

Rows 5–14: [Rep rows 3 and 4 alternately] 5 times.

Row 15: Rep row 3.

Row 16: Sk first st, sl st loosely in each of next 2 sc, sc in next st and in each across, leaving last 3 sts unworked, turn. *(54 sc)*

Rows 17–23: Sk first st, sl st in each of next 2 sts, sc in next st and in each st across, leaving last 3 sts unworked, turn. *(12 sc at end of last row)*

Rows 24–32: Ch 1, sc in each st across, turn. At end of last row, fasten off.

FRONT
RIBBING

Row 1: Ch 9, sc in 2nd ch from hook and in each ch across, turn. *(8 sc)*

Rows 2–18: Working in back lps, ch 1, sc in each st across, turn. At end of last row, **do not turn**.

BODY

Row 1: Working in ends of rows on Ribbing, ch 1, sc in each row across, turn. *(18 sc)*

Row 2: Ch 1, sc in each of first 5 sts, 2 sc in next st, [sc in each of next 5 sts, 2 sc in next st] across, turn. *(21 sc)*

Rows 3–15: [Rep rows 3 and 4 of Back Body alternately] 7 times, ending last rep with row 3.

Row 16: Ch 1, sc in each st across, turn.

Row 17: Ch 1, **sc dec** *(see Stitch Guide)* in first 2 sts, sc in each st across, ending with sc dec in last 2 sts, turn. *(19 sc)*

Row 18: Ch 1, sc in each st across, turn.

Rows 19–24: [Rep rows 17 and 18 alternately] 3 times. *(13 sc at end of last row)*

Row 25: Ch 1, sc in each of first 6 sts, sc dec in next 2 sts, sc in each st across, turn. *(12 sc)*

Rows 26–32: Ch 1, sc in each st across, turn. At end of last row, fasten off.

ASSEMBLY

Sew side edges of Front to Back from Ribbing to row 16 of Body.

Sew last row of Front and Back tog for crotch.

LEG

Rnd 1: Evenly sp 54 sc around Leg opening, **do not join** *(see Pattern Notes)*.

Rnd 2: Sc in each st around.

Rnd 3: [Sc in each of next 7 sts, sc dec in next 2 sts] around. *(48 sc)*

Rnd 4: [Sc in each of next 6 sts, sc dec in next 2 sts] around. *(42 sc)*

Rnds 5–7: Sc in each st around.

At end of last rnd, join in next st. Fasten off.

Rep on rem Leg opening.

HAT
RIBBING

Row 1: Ch 13, sc in 2nd ch from hook and in each ch across, turn. *(12 sc)*

Rows 2–78: Working in **back lps** *(see Stitch Guide)*, ch 1, sc in each st across, turn. At end of last row, **do not turn**.

TOP SECTION

Row 1: Working in ends of rows, ch 1, sc in each row across, turn.

Row 2: **Ch 2** *(see Pattern Notes)*, dc in each st across, turn.

Row 3: Ch 1, sc in each st across, turn.

Rows 4–11: [Rep rows 2 and 3 alternately] 4 times.

Row 12: Ch 2, dc in each of next 10 sts, **dc dec** *(see Stitch Guide)* in next 2 sts, [dc in each of next 11 sts, dc dec in next 2 sts] across. *(72 dc)*

Row 13: Ch 1, sc in each of first 10 sts, **sc dec** *(see Stitch Guide)* in next 2 sts, [sc in each of next 10 sts, sc dec in next 2 sts] across. *(66 sc)*

Row 14: Ch 2, dc in each of next 8 sts, dc dec in next 2 sts, [dc in each of next 9 sts, dc dec in next 2 sts] across. *(60 dc)*

Row 15: Ch 1, sc in each of first 8 sts, sc dec in next 2 sts, [sc in each of next 8 sts, sc dec in next 2 sts] across. *(54 sc)*

Row 16: Ch 2, dc in each of next 6 sts, dc dec in next 2 sts, [dc in each of next 7 sts, dc dec in next 2 sts] across. *(48 dc)*

Row 17: Ch 1, sc in each of first 6 sts, sc dec in next 2 sts, [sc in each of next 6 sts, sc dec in next 2 sts] across. *(42 sc)*

Row 18: Ch 2, dc in each of next 4 sts, dc dec in next 2 sts, [dc in each of next 5 sts, dc dec in next 2 sts] across. *(36 dc)*

Row 19: Ch 1, sc in each of first 4 sts, sc dec in next 2 sts, [sc in each of next 4 sts, sc dec in next 2 sts] across. *(30 sc)*

Row 20: Ch 2, dc in each of next 2 sts, dc dec in next 2 sts, [dc in each of next 3 sts, dc dec in next 2 sts] across. *(24 dc)*

Row 21: Ch 1, sc in each of first 2 sts, sc dec in next 2 sts, [sc in each of next 2 sts, sc dec in next 2 sts] across. *(18 sc)*

Row 22: Ch 2, dc dec in next 2 sts, [dc in next st, dc dec in next 2 sts] across. *(12 dc)*

Row 23: Ch 1, [sc dec in next 2 sts] across. Leaving long end, fasten off.

Weave long end through top of sts on last row, pull to close. Secure end.

Sew ends of rows tog for back seam.

FLOWER

MAKE 2.

Rnd 1: Ch 5, sl st in first ch to form ring, [ch 3, 4 dc in ring, ch 3, sl st in ring] 5 times, **do not join**.

Rnd 2: [3 sc in next ch sp, sc in each of next 4 sts, 3 sc in next ch sp, sl st in next sl st] around.

Rnd 3: [Sc in each of next 3 sts, hdc in next st, 2 hdc in each of next 2 sts, hdc in next st, sc in each of next 3 sts, sl st in next sl st] around.

Rnd 4: [Sc in each of next 3 sts, hdc in each of next 2 sts, 2 dc in each of next 2 sts, hdc in each of next 2 sts, sc in each of next 3 sts, sl st in next sl st] around.

Rnd 5: [Sc in each of next 5 sts, hdc in next st, 3 dc in each of next 2 sts, hdc in next st, sc in each of next 5 sts, sl st in next sl st] around.

Rnd 6: [Sc in next st, hdc in each of next 5 sts, 2 dc in each of next 6 sts, hdc in each of next 5 sts, sc in next st, sl st in next sl st] around, join in next sc. Leaving long end, fasten off.

Sew 1 Flower to Hat and 1 Flower to Diaper Cover as shown in photo. ■

Star Spangled

SKILL LEVEL

INTERMEDIATE

FINISHED SIZES

Newborn–3 months, 3–6 months and 9 months–1 year

MATERIALS

- Cascade Yarn Fixation fine (sport) weight elastic yarn (1¾ oz/100 yds/ 50g per ball):
  1 ball each #9398 hot pink, #8001 opulent white and #9045 stonewash
- Size crochet hook needed for size and gauge
- Tapestry needle
- Stitch marker

2 FINE

GAUGE

Newborn–3 months, size C/2/2.75mm hook: 7 dc = 1 inch

3–6 months, size D/3/3.25mm hook: 6 dc = 1 inch

9 months–1 year, size E/4/3.5mm: 5 dc = 1 inch

Take time to check gauge.

PATTERN NOTES

If using a different yarn, make sure it will stretch and also hold original shape and size, in order to fit properly over diaper.

Chain-2 at beginning of row or round counts as first double crochet unless otherwise stated.

Join with slip stitch as indicated unless otherwise stated.

Work in continuous rounds, do not turn or join unless otherwise stated.

Mark first stitch of round.

INSTRUCTIONS
DIAPER COVER
BACK
RIBBING

Row 1: With hot pink, ch 9, sc in 2nd ch from hook and in each ch across, turn. *(8 sc)*

Rows 2–54: Working in **back lps** *(see Stitch Guide)*, ch 1, sc in each st across, turn. At end of last row, **do not turn**.

BODY

Row 1: Working in ends of rows on Ribbing, ch 1, sc in each row across, turn. *(54 sc)*

Row 2: Working in both lps, ch 1, sc in each of first 8 sts, 2 sc in next st, [sc in each of next 8 sts, 2 sc in next st] across, turn. Fasten off. *(60 sc)*

Row 3: Join *(see Pattern Notes)* opulent white in first st, **ch 2** *(see Pattern Notes)*, dc in each st across, turn.

Row 4: Ch 1, sc in each st across, turn. Fasten off.

Rows 5 & 6: With hot pink, rep rows 3 and 4.

Rows 7–15: [Rep rows 3–6 consecutively] 3 times, ending with row 3.

Row 16: Sk first st, loosely sl st in each of next 2 sts, sc in each of last 54 sts, leaving last 3 sts unworked, turn. Fasten off. *(54 sc)*

Row 17: Join hot pink in 2nd st, loosely sl st in each of next 2 sts, sc in each st across, leaving last 3 sc unworked, turn. *(48 sc)*

Row 18: Sk first st, loosely sl st in each of next 2 sts, sc in each st across, leaving last 3 sc unworked, turn. *(42 sc)*

Row 19: Sk first st, loosely sl st in each of next 2 sts, sc in each st across, leaving last 3 sc unworked, turn. Fasten off. *(36 sc)*

Row 20: Join opulent white in 2nd st, loosely sl st in each of next 2 sts, sc in each st across, leaving last 3 sc unworked, turn. *(30 sc)*

Row 21: Rep row 18. *(24 sc)*

Row 22: Rep row 19. *(18 sc)*

Row 23: Join hot pink in 2nd st, loosely sl st in each of next 2 sts, sc in each st across, leaving last 3 sc unworked, turn. *(12 sc)*

Rows 24 & 25: Ch 1, sc in each st across, turn. At end of last row, fasten off.

Row 26: Join opulent white with sc in first st, sc in each st across, turn.

Rows 27 & 28: Ch 1, sc in each st across, turn. At end of last row, fasten off.

Row 29: Join hot pink with sc in first st, sc in each st across, turn.

Rows 30–32: Ch 1, sc in each st across, turn. At end of last row, fasten off.

FRONT
RIBBING

Row 1: With stonewash, ch 9, sc in 2nd ch from hook and in each ch across, turn. *(8 sc)*

Rows 2–18: Working in back lps, ch 1, sc in each st across, turn. At end of last row, **do not turn**.

BODY

Row 1: Working in ends of rows on Ribbing, ch 1, sc in each row across, turn. *(18 sc)*

Row 2: Ch 1, sc in each of first 5 sts, 2 sc in next st, [sc in each of next 5 sts, 2 sc in next st] across, turn. *(21 sc)*

Row 3: Ch 2, dc in each st across, turn.

Row 4: Ch 1, sc in each st across, turn.

Rows 5–15: [Rep rows 4 and 5 of Back Body alternately] 6 times, ending last rep with row 4.

Row 16: Ch 1, sc in each st across, turn.

Row 17: Ch 1, **sc dec** *(see Stitch Guide)* in first 2 sts, sc in each st across, ending with sc dec in last 2 sts, turn. *(19 sc)*

Row 18: Ch 1, sc in each st across, turn.

Rows 19–24: [Rep rows 17 and 18 alternately] 3 times. *(13 sc at end of last row)*

Row 25: Ch 1, sc in each of first 6 sts, sc dec in next 2 sts, sc in each st across, turn. *(12 sc)*

Rows 26–32: Ch 1, sc in each st across, turn. At end of last row, fasten off.

ASSEMBLY

Sew side edges of Front to Back from Ribbing to top of row 16 of Body.

Sew last row of Front and Back tog for crotch.

LEG

Rnd 1: With hot pink, evenly sp 54 sc around Leg opening, **do not join** *(see Pattern Notes).*

Rnd 2: Sc in each st around.

Rnd 3: [Sc in each of next 7 sts, sc dec in next 2 sts] around. *(48 sc)*

Rnd 4: Sc in each of next 6 sts, sc dec in next 2 sts, [sc in each of next 6 sts, sc dec in next 2 sts] around. *(42 sc)*

Rnds 5 & 6: Sc in each st around. At end of last rnd, join in next st. Fasten off.

Rep on rem Leg opening.

STAR

Rnd 1: With opulent white, ch 2, 5 sc in 2nd ch from hook, **do not join**. *(5 sc)*

Rnd 2: 2 sc in each st around. *(10 sc)*

Rnd 3: [Sc in next st, 2 sc in next st] around. *(15 sc)*

Rnd 4: Sl st in first sc, *ch 5, sc in 2nd ch from hook, hdc in next ch, dc in next ch, tr in last ch, sk next 2 sts on rnd 3**, sl st in next st, rep from * around, ending last rep at **, join in beg sl st. Fasten off.

Sew Star to Cover Front as shown in photo.

STAR-SPANGLED HAT

RIBBING

Row 1: With opulent white, ch 13, sc in 2nd ch from hook and in each ch across, turn. *(12 sc)*

Rows 2–78: Working in **back lps** *(see Stitch Guide)*, ch 1, sc in each st across, turn. At end of last row, **do not turn**.

TOP SECTION

Row 1: Working in ends of rows, ch 1, sc in each row across, turn. *(78 sc)*

Row 2: Ch 2, dc in each st across, turn. Fasten off.

Row 3: Join hot pink with sc in first st, sc in each st across, turn. Fasten off.

Row 4: Join stonewash in first st, ch 2, dc in each st across, turn.

Row 5: Ch 1, sc in each st across, turn.

Row 6: **Ch 2** *(see Pattern Notes)*, dc in each st across, turn.

Rows 7–10: [Rep rows 5 and 6 alternately] twice. At end of last row, fasten off.

Row 11: Rep row 3.

Row 12: Join opulent white in first st, ch 2, dc in each of next 10 sts, **dc dec** *(see Stitch Guide)* in next 2 sts, [dc in each of next 11 sts, dc dec in next 2 sts] across, turn. *(72 dc)*

Row 13: Ch 1, sc in each of first 10 sts, **sc dec** *(see Stitch Guide)* in next 2 sts, [sc in each of next 10 sts, sc dec in next 2 sts] across, turn. *(66 sc)*

Row 14: Ch 2, dc in each of next 8 sts, dc dec in next 2 sts, [dc in each of next 9 sts, dc dec in next 2 sts] across, turn. *(60 dc)*

Row 15: Ch 1, sc in each of first 8 sts, sc dec in next 2 sts, [sc in each of next 8 sts, sc dec in next 2 sts] across, turn. *(54 sc)*

Row 16: Ch 2, dc in each of next 6 sts, dc dec in next 2 sts, [dc in each of next 7 sts, dc dec in next 2 sts] across, turn. *(48 dc)*

Row 17: Ch 1, sc in each of first 6 sts, sc dec in next 2 sts, [sc in each of next 6 sts, sc dec in next 2 sts] across, turn. *(42 sc)*

Row 18: Ch 2, dc in each of next 4 sts, dc dec in next 2 sts, [dc in each of next 5 sts, dc dec in next 2 sts] across, turn. *(36 dc)*

Row 19: Ch 1, sc in each of first 4 sts, sc dec in next 2 sts, [sc in each of next 4 sts, sc dec in next 2 sts] across, turn. *(30 sc)*

Row 20: Ch 2, dc in each of next 2 sts, dc dec in next 2 sts, [dc in each of next 3 sts, dc dec in next 2 sts] across, turn. *(24 dc)*

Row 21: Ch 1, sc in each of first 2 sts, sc dec in next 2 sts, [sc in each of next 2 sts, sc dec in next 2 sts] across, turn. *(18 sc)*

Row 22: Ch 2, dc dec in next 2 sts, [dc in next st, dc dec in next 2 sts] around. *(12 dc)*

Row 23: Ch 1, [sc dec in next 2 sts] across. Leaving long end, fasten off.

Weave long end through top of sts on last row, pull to close. Secure end.

Sew ends of rows tog for back seam.

STAR

Rnd 1: With opulent white, ch 2, 5 sc in 2nd ch from hook, **do not join.** *(5 sc)*

Rnd 2: 2 sc in each st around. *(10 sc)*

Rnd 3: [Sl st in next st, ch 4, sc in 2nd ch from hook, hdc in next ch, dc in next ch] around, join in beg sl st. Fasten off.

Sew Star to Hat as shown in photo. ■

Sunshine & Flowers

SKILL LEVEL

INTERMEDIATE

FINISHED SIZES

Newborn–3 months, 3–6 months and 9 months–1 year

MATERIALS

- Cascade Yarn Fixation fine (sport) weight elastic yarn (1¾ oz/100 yds/ 50g per ball):
  1 ball each #1198 light yellow
  #8001 opulent white
- Size crochet hook needed for size and gauge
- Tapestry needle

2 FINE

GAUGE

Newborn–3 months, size C/2/2.75mm hook: 7 dc = 1 inch
3–6 months, size D/3/3.25mm hook: 6 dc = 1 inch
9 months–1 year, size E/4/3.5mm: 5 dc = 1 inch
Take time to check gauge.

PATTERN NOTES

If using a different yarn, make sure it will stretch and also hold original shape and size, in order to fit properly over diaper.

Chain-2 at beginning of row or round counts as first double crochet unless otherwise stated.

Join with slip stitch as indicated unless otherwise stated.

INSTRUCTIONS
DIAPER COVER
BACK
RIBBING

Row 1: With light yellow, ch 9, sc in 2nd ch from hook and in each ch across, turn. *(8 sc)*

Rows 2–54: Working in **back lps** *(see Stitch Guide)*, ch 1, sc in each st across, turn. At end of last row, **do not turn.**

BODY

Row 1: Working in ends of rows on Ribbing, ch 1, sc in each row across, turn. *(54 sc)*

Row 2: Working in both lps, ch 1, sc in each of first 8 sts, 2 sc in next st, [sc in each of next 8 sts, 2 sc in next st] across, turn. *(60 sc)*

Row 3: **Ch 2** *(see Pattern Notes)*, dc in each st across, turn.

Row 4: Ch 1, sc in each st across, turn.

Rows 5–14: [Rep rows 3 and 4 alternately] 5 times.

Row 15: Rep row 3.

Row 16: Sk first st, loosely sl st in each of next 2 sts, sc in each of last 54 sts, leaving last 3 sts unworked, turn. *(54 sc)*

Rows 17–23: Sk first st, loosely sl st in each of next 2 sts, sc in each st across, leaving last 3 sc unworked, turn. *(12 sc at end of last row)*

Rows 24–32: Ch 1, sc in each st across, turn. At end of last row, fasten off.

FRONT
RIBBING

Row 1: With opulent white, ch 9, sc in 2nd ch from hook and in each ch across, turn. *(8 sc)*

Rows 2–18: Working in back lps, ch 1, sc in each st across, turn. At end of last row, **do not turn.**

BODY

Row 1: Working in ends of rows on Ribbing, ch 1, sc in each row across, turn. *(18 sc)*

Row 2: Ch 1, sc in each of first 5 sts, 2 sc in next st, [sc in each of next 5 sts, 2 sc in next st] across, turn. *(21 sc)*

Rows 3–15: [Rep rows 3 and 4 of Back Body alternately] 7 times, ending last rep with row 3.

Row 16: Ch 1, sc in each st across, turn.

Row 17: Ch 1, **sc dec** *(see Stitch Guide)* in first 2 sts, sc in each st across, ending with sc dec in last 2 sts, turn. *(19 sc)*

Row 18: Ch 1, sc in each st across, turn.

Rows 19–24: [Rep rows 17 and 18 alternately] 3 times. *(13 sc at end of last row)*

Row 25: Ch 1, sc in each of first 6 sts, sc dec in next 2 sts, sc in each st across, turn. *(12 sc)*

Rows 26–32: Ch 1, sc in each st across, turn. At end of last row, fasten off.

ASSEMBLY

Sew side edges of Front to Back from Ribbing to top of row 16 of Body.

Sew last rows of Front and Back tog for crotch.

TIE
MAKE 2.

With light yellow, ch 50, sl st in 2nd ch from hook and in each ch across. Fasten off.

Sew 1 Tie to each side of Back under Ribbing.

Weave Tie through sts to center Back.

Tie ends in bow.

LEG

Rnd 1: With light yellow, evenly sp 54 sc around Leg opening, **do not join.**

Rnd 2: Sc in each st around.

Rnd 3: [Sc in each of next 7 sts, sc dec in next 2 sts] around. Fasten off. *(48 sc)*

Rnd 4: Join opulent white with sc in first st, sc in each of next 5 sts, sc dec in next 2 sts, [sc in each of next 6 sts, sc dec in next 2 sts] around. *(42 sc)*

Rnd 5: Sc in each st around.

Rnd 6: Ch 2, 2 dc in same st, 3 dc in each st around.

Rnd 7: Sl st in first st, ch 3, sk next st, [sl st in next st, ch 3, sk next st] around, **join** *(see Pattern Notes)* in beg sl st. Fasten off.

Rep on rem Leg opening.

FLOWER

Rnd 1: With light yellow, ch 6, sl st in first ch to form ring, ch 1, 12 sc in ring, **do not join.**

Rnd 2: Working in **front lps** *(see Stitch Guide),* 2 sc in each st around. *(24 sc)*

Rnd 3: Working in both lps, [sc in next st, (hdc, 2 dc) in next st, (2 dc, hdc) in next st, sc in next st] around, join in beg sc, ch 2, sl st in back lp of next st. *(6 petals)*

Rnd 4: Working in rem lps of rnd 1, ch 2, 2 sc in same st, 2 sc in each st around. *(24 sc)*

Rnd 5: Sc in each st around.

Rnd 6: [Sc in next st, (hdc, dc, tr) in next st, (tr, dc, hdc) in next st, sc in next st] around, join in beg sc. Fasten off.

Sew to Front of Cover.

HEADBAND

Row 1: With opulent white, ch 5, sc in 2nd ch from hook and in each ch across, turn. *(4 sc)*

Rows 2–64: Working in **back lps** *(see Stitch Guide),* ch 1, sc in each st across, turn. The size of Headband can be changed to fit any baby by working more or less rows. At end of last row, fasten off.

Sew first and last rows tog to form circle.

LARGE FLOWER

Rnd 1: With light yellow, ch 2, 6 sc in 2nd ch from hook, **do not join.** *(6 sc)*

Rnd 2: Working in **front lps** *(see Stitch Guide),* 2 sc in each st around. *(12 sc)*

Rnd 3: Working in back lps of rnd 1, sl st in back lp of next st, **ch 2** *(see Pattern Notes),* 2 dc in same st, 3 dc in each st around.

Rnd 4: Ch 2, sk next st, [sl st in next st, ch 2] around, join in base of beg ch-2. Fasten off.

SMALL FLOWER
MAKE 2.

Rnd 1: With light yellow, ch 2, 6 sc in 2nd ch from hook, **do not join.** *(6 sc)*

Rnd 2: (Sl st, ch 1, hdc, ch 1, sl st) in each st around, join in beg sl st. Fasten off.

Sew Flowers to Headband as shown in photo. ■

Teddy Bear

SKILL LEVEL

INTERMEDIATE

FINISHED SIZES

Newborn–3 months, 3–6 months and 9 months–1 year

MATERIALS

- Cascade Yarn Fixation fine (sport) weight elastic yarn (1¾ oz/100 yds/50g per ball):
  - 2 balls #9442 Hawaiian
  - 1 ball each #7382 chocolate, #8176 ecru and #8001 opulent white
- Size 8 pearl cotton:
  - 10 yds each blue, black and brown
- Size crochet hook needed for size and gauge
- Tapestry needle
- Stitch marker

GAUGE

Newborn–3 months, size C/2/2.75mm hook: 7 dc = 1 inch

3–6 months, size D/3/3.25mm hook: 6 dc = 1 inch

9 months–1 year, size E/4/3.5mm: 5 dc = 1 inch

Take time to check gauge.

PATTERN NOTES

If using a different yarn, make sure it will stretch and also hold original shape and size, in order to fit properly over diaper.

Chain-2 at beginning of row or round counts as first double crochet unless otherwise stated.

Work in continuous rounds, do not turn or join unless otherwise stated.

Mark first stitch of each round.

Join with slip stitch as indicated unless otherwise stated.

INSTRUCTIONS

DIAPER COVER

BACK

RIBBING

Row 1: With Hawaiian, ch 9, sc in 2nd ch from hook and in each ch across, turn. *(8 sc)*

Rows 2–54: Working in **back lps** *(see Stitch Guide)*, ch 1, sc in each st across, turn. At end of last row, **do not turn**.

BODY

Row 1: Working in ends of rows on Ribbing, ch 1, sc in each row across, turn. *(54 sc)*

Row 2: Working in both lps, ch 1, sc in each of first 8 sts, 2 sc in next st, [sc in each of next 8 sts, 2 sc in next st] across, turn. *(60 sc)*

Row 3: Ch 2 *(see Pattern Notes)*, dc in each st across, turn.

Row 4: Ch 1, sc in each st across, turn.

Rows 5–14: [Rep rows 3 and 4 alternately] 5 times.

Row 15: Rep row 3.

Row 16: Sk first st, loosely sl st in each of next 2 sts, sc in each of next 54 sts, leaving last 3 sts unworked, turn. *(54 sc)*

Rows 17–23: Sk first st, loosely sl st in each of next 2 sts, sc in each st across, leaving last 3 sc unworked, turn. *(12 sc at end of last row)*

Rows 24–32: Ch 1, sc in each st across, turn. At end of last row, fasten off.

FRONT

RIBBING

Row 1: With Hawaiian, ch 9, sc in 2nd ch from hook and in each ch across, turn. *(8 sc)*

Rows 2–18: Working in back lps, ch 1, sc in each st across, turn. At end of last row, **do not turn**.

BODY

Row 1: Working in ends of rows on Ribbing, ch 1, sc in each row across, turn. *(18 sc)*

Row 2: Ch 1, sc in each of first 5 sts, 2 sc in next st, [sc in each of next 5 sts, 2 sc in next st] across, turn. Fasten off. *(21 sc)*

Row 3: Join *(see Pattern Notes)* opulent white in first st, ch 2, dc in each st across, turn.

Rows 4–12: [Rep rows 4 and 3 of Back Body alternately] 5 times, ending last rep with row 4. At end of last row, fasten off.

Row 13: Join Hawaiian in first st, ch 2, dc in each st across, turn.

Row 14: Rep row 4 of Back

Row 15: Rep row 3 of Back.

Row 16: Ch 1, sc in each st across, turn.

Row 17: Ch 1, **sc dec** *(see Stitch Guide)* in first 2 sts, sc in each st across, ending with sc dec in last 2 sts, turn. *(19 sc)*

Row 18: Ch 1, sc in each st across, turn.

Rows 19–24: [Rep rows 17 and 18 alternately] 3 times. *(13 sc at end of last row)*

Row 25: Ch 1, sc in each of first 6 sts, sc dec in next 2 sts, sc in each st across, turn. *(12 sc)*

Rows 26–32: Ch 1, sc in each st across, turn. At end of last row, fasten off.

ASSEMBLY

Sew side edges of Front to Back from Ribbing to top of row 16 of Body.

Sew last row of Front and Back tog for crotch.

LEG

Rnd 1: With Hawaiian, evenly sp 54 sc around Leg opening, **do not join** *(see Pattern Notes)*.

Rnd 2: Sc in each st around.

Rnd 3: [Sc in each of next 7 sts, sc dec in next 2 sts] around. *(48 sc)*

Rnd 4: [Sc in each of next 6 sts, sc dec in next 2 sts] around. *(42 sc)*

Rnds 5 & 6: Sc in each st around. At end of last rnd, fasten off.

Rep on Leg opening.

BEAR
HEAD

Rnd 1: With chocolate, ch 2, 6 sc in 2nd ch from hook, **do not join**. *(6 sc)*

Rnd 2: 2 sc in each st around. *(12 sc)*

Rnd 3: [Sc in next st, 2 sc in next st] around. *(18 sc)*

Rnd 4: [Sc in each of next 2 sts, 2 sc in next st] around. *(24 sc)*

Rnd 5: [Sc in each of next 3 sts, 2 sc in next st] around, join in next st. Fasten off. *(30 sc)*

SNOUT

Rnd 1: With ecru, ch 2, 6 sc in 2nd ch from hook, **do not join**. *(6 sc)*

Rnd 2: 2 sc in each st around, join in next st. Fasten off. *(12 sc)*

EAR
MAKE 2.

Row 1: With chocolate, ch 2, 5 sc in 2nd ch from hook, turn. *(5 sc)*

Row 2: 2 sc in each st across. Fasten off. *(10 sc)*

ASSEMBLY

Using **satin stitch** *(see Fig. 1)*, with brown pearl cotton, embroider nose on Snout as shown in photo.

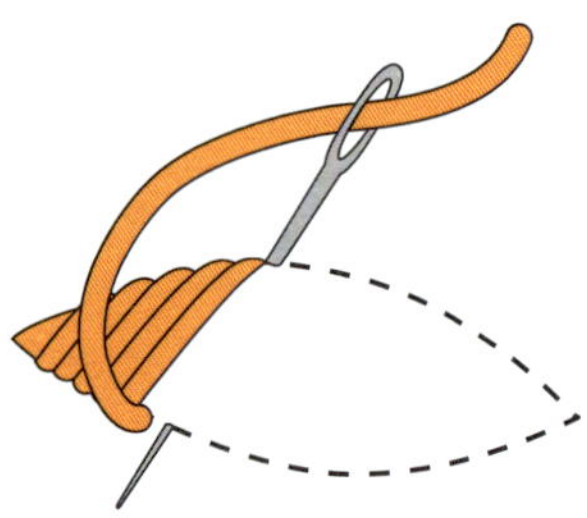

Fig. 1
Satin Stitch

Using **straight stitch** *(see Fig 2.)*, with brown pearl cotton, embroider mouth to Snout centered below nose as shown in photo.

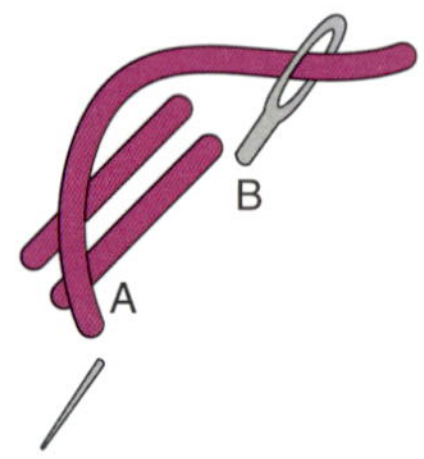

Fig. 2
Straight Stitch

Sew Snout to Head as shown in photo.

Using **French knots** *(see Fig. 3)*, with blue pearl cotton, embroider eyes on Head above Snout as shown in photo.

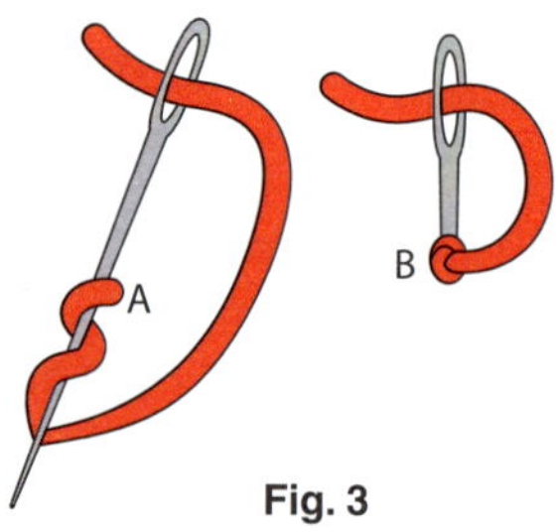

Fig. 3
French Knot

Sew Head to white section on Front of Diaper Cover as shown in photo.

Sew 1 Ear to each side of Head as shown in photo.

HAT
RIBBING

Row 1: With Hawaiian, ch 13, sc in 2nd ch from hook and in each ch across, turn. *(12 sc)*

Rows 2–78: Working in **back lps** *(see Stitch Guide)*, ch 1, sc in each st across, turn. At end of last row, **do not turn**.

TOP SECTION

Row 1: Working in ends of rows, ch 1, sc in each row across, turn. Fasten off. *(78 sc)*

Row 2: Join chocolate in first st, **ch 2** *(see Pattern Notes)*, dc in each st across, turn.

Row 3: Ch 1, sc in each st across, turn.

Rows 4–11: [Rep rows 2 and 3 alternately] 4 times.

Row 12: Ch 2, dc in each of next 10 sts, **dc dec** *(see Stitch Guide)* in next 2 sts, [dc in each of next 11 sts, dc dec in next 2 sts] across, turn. *(72 dc)*

Row 13: Ch 1, sc in each of first 10 sts, **sc dec** *(see Stitch Guide)* in next 2 sts, [sc in each of next 10 sts, sc dec in next 2 sts] across, turn. *(66 sc)*

Row 14: Ch 2, dc in each of next 8 sts, dc dec in next 2 sts, [dc in each of next 9 sts, dc dec in next 2 sts] across, turn. *(60 dc)*

Row 15: Ch 1, sc in each of first 8 sts, sc dec in next 2 sts, [sc in each of next 8 sts, sc dec in next 2 sts] across, turn. *(54 sc)*

Row 16: Ch 2, dc in each of next 6 sts, dc dec in next 2 sts, [dc in each of next 7 sts, dc dec in next 2 sts] across, turn. *(48 dc)*

Row 17: Ch 1, sc in each of first 6 sts, sc dec in next 2 sts, [sc in each of next 6 sts, sc dec in next 2 sts] across, turn. *(42 sc)*

Row 18: Ch 2, dc in each of next 4 sts, dc dec in next 2 sts, [dc in each of next 5 sts, dc dec in next 2 sts] across, turn. *(36 dc)*

Row 19: Ch 1, sc in each of first 4 sts, sc dec in next 2 sts, [sc in each of next 4 sts, sc dec in next 2 sts] across, turn. *(30 sc)*

Row 20: Ch 2, dc in each of next 2 sts, dc dec in next 2 sts, [dc in each of next 3 sts, dc dec in next 2 sts] across, turn. *(24 dc)*

Row 21: Ch 1, sc in each of first 2 sts, sc dec in next 2 sts, [sc in each of next 2 sts, sc dec in next 2 sts] across, turn. *(18 sc)*

Row 22: Ch 2, dc dec in next 2 sts, [dc in next st, dc dec in next 2 sts] across, turn. *(12 dc)*

Row 23: Ch 1, [sc dec in next 2 sts] across. Leaving long end, fasten off. *(6 sc)*

Weave long end through top of sts on last row, pull to close. Secure end.

Sew ends of rows tog for back seam.

EAR

MAKE 2.

Row 1: With chocolate, ch 2, 5 sc in 2nd ch from hook, turn. *(5 sc)*

Row 2: Ch 2, dc in same st, 2 dc in each st across, turn. *(10 dc)*

Row 3: Ch 1, sc in first st, 2 sc in next st, [sc in next st, 2 sc in next st] across, turn. *(15 sc)*

Row 4: Ch 2, dc in next st, 2 dc in next st, [dc in each of next 2 sts, 2 dc in next st] across, turn. *(20 dc)*

Row 5: Working in back lps, ch 1, sc in each st across, turn.

Row 6: Ch 2, dc in next st, dc dec in next 2 sts, [dc in each of next 2 sts, dc dec in next 2 sts] across, turn. *(15 dc)*

Row 7: [Sc in next st, sc dec in next 2 sts] across, turn. *(10 sc)*

Row 8: Ch 1, dc dec in first 2 sts, [dc dec in next 2 sts] across, turn. *(5 dc)*

Row 9: Ch 1, sc dec in next 5 sts. Leaving long end, fasten off.

Fold Ear in half and sew Ears to Top Section of Hat as shown in photo.

SNOUT

Rnd 1: With ecru, ch 2, 6 sc in 2nd ch from hook, **do not join.** *(6 sc)*

Rnd 2: 2 sc in each st around. *(12 sc)*

Rnd 3: [Sc in next st, 2 sc in next st] around. *(18 sc)*

Rnd 4: [Sc in each of next 2 sts, 2 sc in next st] around. *(24 sc)*

Rnd 5: [Sc in each of next 3 sts, 2 sc in next st] around. *(30 sc)*

Rnd 6: [Sc in each of next 4 sts, 2 sc in next st] around. *(36 sc)*

Rnd 7: [Sc in each of next 5 sts, 2 sc in next st] around, join in next st. Fasten off. *(42 sc)*

FINISHING

Using satin stitch, with brown pearl cotton, embroider nose on Snout as shown in photo.

Using straight stitch, with brown pearl cotton, embroider mouth on Snout as shown in photo.

Sew Snout in place on Top Section of Hat between Ears.

Using satin stitch, with blue pearl cotton, embroider eyes above and on each side of Snout.

Using French knot, with black, embroider 1 French knot to top of each eye as shown in photo. ■

Stitch Guide

For more complete information, visit **FreePatterns.com**

ABBREVIATIONS

beg	begin/begins/beginning
bpdc	back post double crochet
bpsc	back post single crochet
bptr	back post treble crochet
CC	contrasting color
ch(s)	chain(s)
ch-	refers to chain or space previously made (e.g., ch-1 space)
ch sp(s)	chain space(s)
cl(s)	cluster(s)
cm	centimeter(s)
dc	double crochet (singular/plural)
dc dec	double crochet 2 or more stitches together, as indicated
dec	decrease/decreases/decreasing
dtr	double treble crochet
ext	extended
fpdc	front post double crochet
fpsc	front post single crochet
fptr	front post treble crochet
g	gram(s)
hdc	half double crochet
hdc dec	half double crochet 2 or more stitches together, as indicated
inc	increase/increases/increasing
lp(s)	loop(s)
MC	main color
mm	millimeter(s)
oz	ounce(s)
pc	popcorn(s)
rem	remain/remains/remaining
rep(s)	repeat(s)
rnd(s)	round(s)
RS	right side
sc	single crochet (singular/plural)
sc dec	single crochet 2 or more stitches together, as indicated
sk	skip/skipped/skipping
sl st(s)	slip stitch(es)
sp(s)	space/spaces/spaced
st(s)	stitch(es)
tog	together
tr	treble crochet
trtr	triple treble
WS	wrong side
yd(s)	yard(s)
yo	yarn over

Chain—ch: Yo, pull through lp on hook.

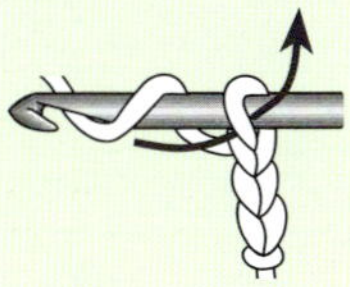

Slip stitch—sl st: Insert hook in st, pull through both lps on hook.

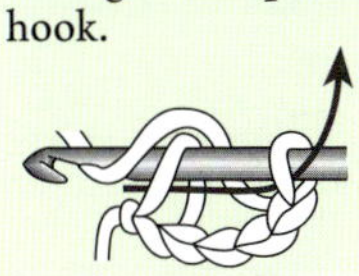

Single crochet—sc: Insert hook in st, yo, pull through st, yo, pull through both lps on hook.

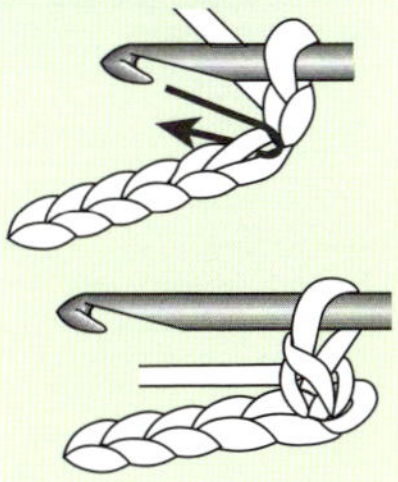

Front post stitch—fp:
Back post stitch—bp: When working post st, insert hook from right to left around post st on previous row.

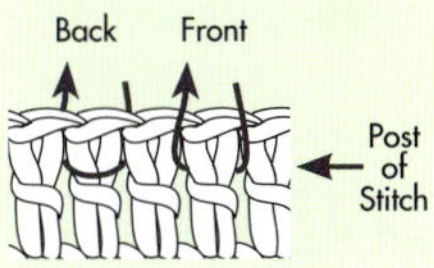

Front loop—front lp
Back loop—back lp

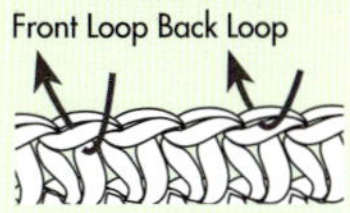

Half double crochet—hdc: Yo, insert hook in st, yo, pull through st, yo, pull through all 3 lps on hook.

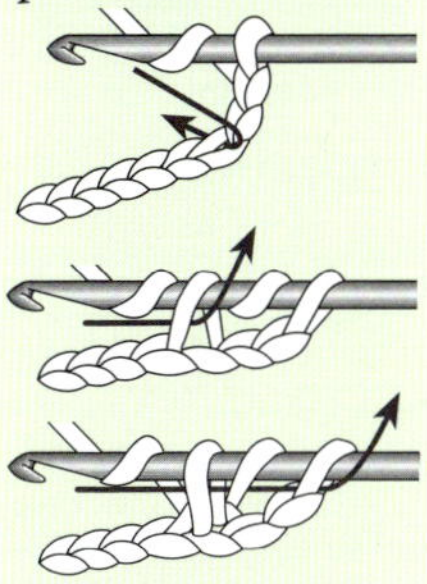

Double crochet—dc: Yo, insert hook in st, yo, pull through st, [yo, pull through 2 lps] twice.

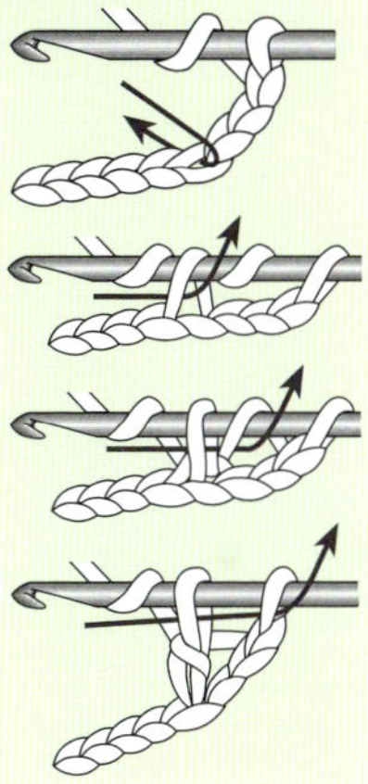

Change colors: Drop first color; with 2nd color, pull through last 2 lps of st.

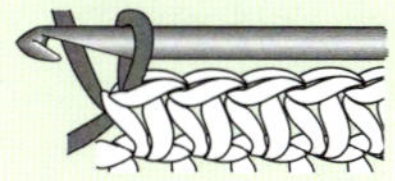

Treble crochet—tr: Yo twice, insert hook in st, yo, pull through st, [yo, pull through 2 lps] 3 times.

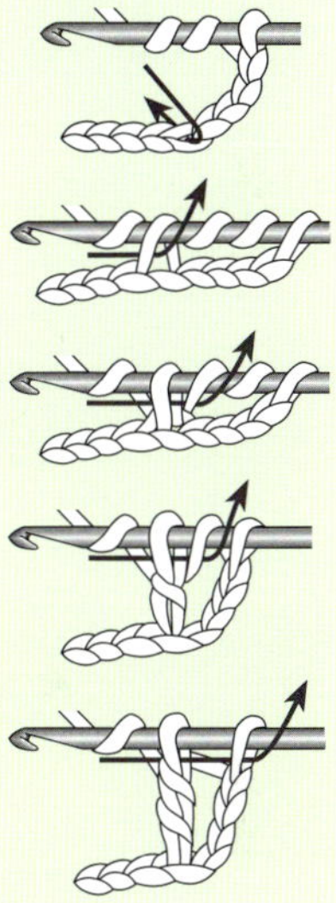

Double treble crochet—dtr: Yo 3 times, insert hook in st, yo, pull through st, [yo, pull through 2 lps] 4 times.

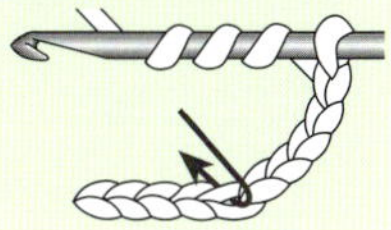

Single crochet decrease (sc dec): (Insert hook, yo, draw lp through) in each of the sts indicated, yo, draw through all lps on hook.

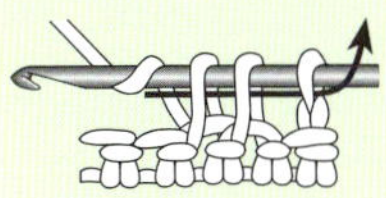

Example of 2-sc dec

Half double crochet decrease (hdc dec): (Yo, insert hook, yo, draw lp through) in each of the sts indicated, yo, draw through all lps on hook.

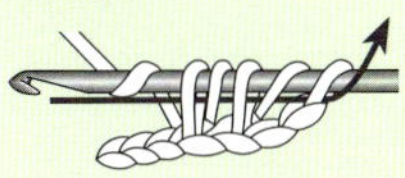

Example of 2-hdc dec

Double crochet decrease (dc dec): (Yo, insert hook, yo, draw loop through, draw through 2 lps on hook) in each of the sts indicated, yo, draw through all lps on hook.

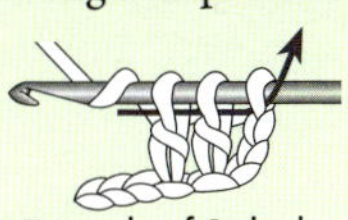

Example of 2-dc dec

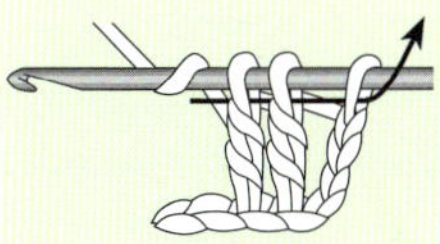

Example of 2-tr dec

Treble crochet decrease (tr dec): Holding back last lp of each st, tr in each of the sts indicated, yo, pull through all lps on hook.

US		UK
sl st (slip stitch)	=	sc (single crochet)
sc (single crochet)	=	dc (double crochet)
hdc (half double crochet)	=	htr (half treble crochet)
dc (double crochet)	=	tr (treble crochet)
tr (treble crochet)	=	dtr (double treble crochet)
dtr (double treble crochet)	=	ttr (triple treble crochet)
skip	=	miss

Metric Conversion Charts

METRIC CONVERSIONS

yards	x	.9144	=	metres (m)
yards	x	91.44	=	centimetres (cm)
inches	x	2.54	=	centimetres (cm)
inches	x	25.40	=	millimetres (mm)
inches	x	.0254	=	metres (m)

centimetres	x	.3937	=	inches
metres	x	1.0936	=	yards

INCHES INTO MILLIMETRES & CENTIMETRES (Rounded off slightly)

inches	mm	cm	inches	cm	inches	cm	inches	cm
1/8	3	0.3	5	12.5	21	53.5	38	96.5
1/4	6	0.6	5 1/2	14	22	56	39	99
3/8	10	1	6	15	23	58.5	40	101.5
1/2	13	1.3	7	18	24	61	41	104
5/8	15	1.5	8	20.5	25	63.5	42	106.5
3/4	20	2	9	23	26	66	43	109
7/8	22	2.2	10	25.5	27	68.5	44	112
1	25	2.5	11	28	28	71	45	114.5
1 1/4	32	3.2	12	30.5	29	73.5	46	117
1 1/2	38	3.8	13	33	30	76	47	119.5
1 3/4	45	4.5	14	35.5	31	79	48	122
2	50	5	15	38	32	81.5	49	124.5
2 1/2	65	6.5	16	40.5	33	84	50	127
3	75	7.5	17	43	34	86.5		
3 1/2	90	9	18	46	35	89		
4	100	10	19	48.5	36	91.5		
4 1/2	115	11.5	20	51	37	94		

KNITTING NEEDLES CONVERSION CHART

Canada/U.S.	0	1	2	3	4	5	6	7	8	9	10	10½	11	13	15
Metric (mm)	2	2¼	2¾	3¼	3½	3¾	4	4½	5	5½	6	6½	8	9	10

CROCHET HOOKS CONVERSION CHART

Canada/U.S.	1/B	2/C	3/D	4/E	5/F	6/G	8/H	9/I	10/J	10½/K	N
Metric (mm)	2.25	2.75	3.25	3.5	3.75	4.25	5	5.5	6	6.5	9.0

TOLL-FREE ORDER LINE or to request a free catalog (800) LV-ANNIE (800) 582-6643
Customer Service (800) AT-ANNIE (800) 282-6643, **Fax** (800) 882-6643
Visit AnniesAttic.com

ISBN: 978-1-59635-299-5

Printed in USA

1 2 3 4 5 6 7 8 9